Americans at War

TIMELINE *of*
WORLD WAR II
PACIFIC

By Charlie Samuels

Gareth Stevens
Publishing

Please visit our website, www.garethstevens.com. For a free color catalog of all our high-quality books, call toll free 1-800-542-2595 or fax 1-877-542-2596.

Library of Congress Cataloging-in-Publication Data
Samuels, Charlie, 1961-
Timeline of World War II. Pacific / Charlie Samuels.
    p. cm. — (Americans at war : a Gareth Stevens timeline series)
Includes bibliographical references and index.
ISBN 978-1-4339-5935-6 (pbk.)
ISBN 978-1-4339-5936-3 (6-pack)
ISBN 978-1-4339-5934-9 (library binding)
1. World War, 1939-1945—Campaigns—Pacific Area—Juvenile literature. 2. World War, 1939-1945—Campaigns—Pacific Area—Chronology—Juvenile literature. I. Title. II. Title: Timeline of World War 2. Pacific. III. Title: Timeline of World War Two. Pacific.
D767.S315 2011
940.54'26—dc22

2010050920

Published in 2012 by
Gareth Stevens Publishing
111 East 14th Street, Suite 349
New York, NY 10003

© 2011 Brown Bear Books Ltd

For Brown Bear Books Ltd:
Editorial Director: Lindsey Lowe
Managing Editor: Tim Cooke
Children's Publisher: Anne O'Daly
Art Director: Jeni Child
Designer: Karen Perry
Picture Manager: Sophie Mortimer
Production Director: Alastair Gourlay

Picture Credits:
Front Cover: Robert Hunt Library

t = top, b = bottom
Corbis: 22; Bettmann 25, 31; Hulton Deutsch 9t; **Getty Images:** MPI 44b; **Lebrecht Collection:** 10, 12t; **Robert Hunt Library:** 6, 8, 9b, 11, 13, 14, 15t, 15b, 16, 17, 18, 19, 21, 24t, 24b, 26, 28, 29t, 29b, 30, 32, 33, 34, 35, 36, 37, 38, 39, 40, 41, 42, 43, 44t, 45; **TopFoto:** 12b

All Artworks © Brown Bear Books Ltd

Publisher's note to educators and parents: Our editors have carefully reviewed the websites that appear on p. 47 to ensure that they are suitable for students. Many websites change frequently, however, and we cannot guarantee that a site's future contents will continue to meet our high standards of quality and educational value. Be advised that students should be closely supervised whenever they access the Internet.

Manufactured in the United States of America
1 2 3 4 5 6 7 8 9 12 11 10

CPSIA compliance information: Batch #CR215210GS : For further information contact Gareth Stevens, New York, New York at 1-800-542-2595.

Contents

Introduction

World War II was the largest and most destructive war in history. Between 1939 and 1945, 100 million troops were mobilized across the world.

In the Pacific, the war ranged from naval battles fought by aircraft flying from carriers that never came within sight of one another to fierce hand-to-hand fighting on the coral islands.

The Course of the War

Japan sought to expand in Southeast Asia to secure supplies of resources such as oil. Its best chance of victory was to knock out the United States before its superior industrial strength could have an impact. The Japanese air strike on Pearl Harbor, Hawaii, in December 1941 achieved complete surprise but failed to strike the decisive blow. Still, Japan's initial advance swept aside Allied resistance and brought much of Southeast Asia under Japanese command, from Burma to the Philippines. The United States was rebuilding its fleet strength, however, and, in a series of naval clashes, won an advantage over the Japanese. That allowed US planners to launch thrusts from island to island across the vast ocean. As US marines made a series of difficult amphibious landings, a combination of aircraft carriers and captured airbases brought US forces within striking distance of Japan itself. Stiff Japanese resistance in the island campaign eventually convinced the US leadership to use the new atomic bomb rather than risk a conventional landing on the home islands.

About This Book

This book focuses on the war in the Pacific from 1941 to 1945. It contains two types of timelines. Along the bottom of the pages is a timeline that covers the whole period. It lists key events and developments, including from Europe and North Africa, color coded. Each chapter also has its own timeline, which runs vertically down the sides of the pages. This timeline gives more specific details about the particular subject of the chapter.

US marines wade ashore from a landing craft in the invasion of Guadalcanal, in the Solomon Islands, in August 1942. ↓

The Approach of War

The Japanese attack on Pearl Harbor on December 7, 1941, stunned the world. In fact, the storm clouds of war had been gathering over the Pacific for two decades.

Japanese troops ⟫ head to China in the 1930s. The Japanese invaded northern China in 1931.

Timeline
1941
November–
December

November

November 26 Pacific Ocean Japanese aircraft carriers set sail for Pearl Harbor, Hawaii. The aim is to destroy US warships in the region and then to seize land in the Pacific and Asia.

Japan's modernization began in 1867. The Meiji Restoration brought the emperors back to the throne and ended centuries of international isolation.

Building Tensions

Japan had joined the Allies (Britain, France, and the United States) in World War I (1914–1918). After Allied victory, however, the peace settlements forced it to give up Chinese territory it had conquered. A later agreement limited the size of Japan's navy in the Pacific. The Japanese believed their former allies were now treating them like a second-class nation. The Japanese also resented the Western powers' Asian colonies. Japan had to import nearly all of its food, metal, and oil. It wanted its own colonies to provide such goods. Prejudice against Japanese immigrants on the US West Coast was another cause of tension between Japan and the United States.

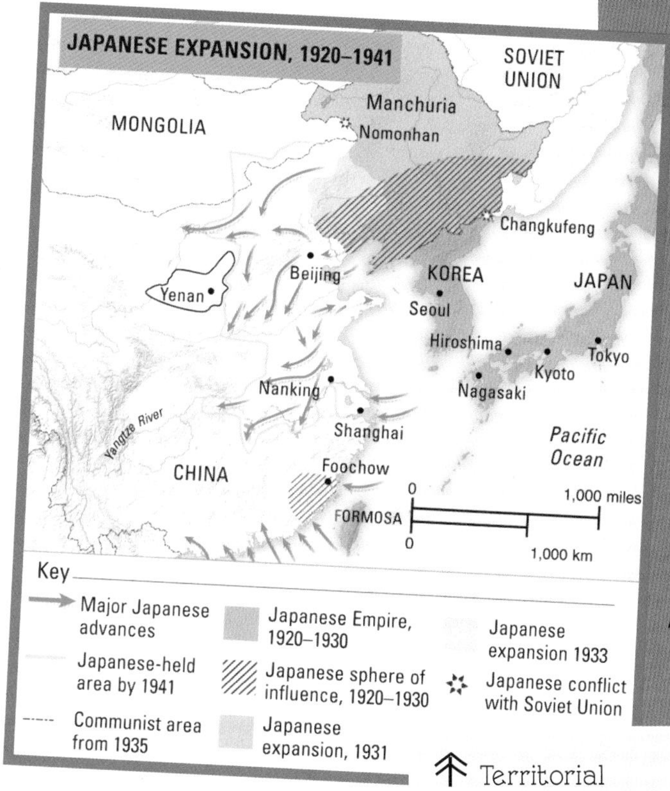
JAPANESE EXPANSION, 1920–1941
SOVIET UNION
MONGOLIA
Manchuria
Nomonhan
Changkufeng
Beijing
Yenan
KOREA
Seoul
JAPAN
Hiroshima
Kyoto
Tokyo
Nagasaki
Nanking
Shanghai
Yangtze River
CHINA
Foochow
FORMOSA
Pacific Ocean
0
1,000 miles
0
1,000 km
Key
Major Japanese advances
Japanese-held area by 1941
Communist area from 1935
Japanese Empire, 1920–1930
Japanese sphere of influence, 1920–1930
Japanese expansion, 1931
Japanese expansion 1933
Japanese conflict with Soviet Union

↑ Territorial expansion was a key part of Japan's long-term modernization.

Timeline

1922 Washington Naval Treaty restricts Japan's naval power in the Pacific.

1924 US Immigration Act stops Japanese immigration to the United States.

1926 Pro-Western Emperor Hirohito comes to the Japanese throne.

1931 Imperial Japanese Army invades Manchuria.

1932 Japan rejects the Washington Naval Treaty.

1933 Japan withdraws from the League of Nations.

1936 Japan negotiates Anti-Comintern Pact with Germany.

July 1937 Start of second Sino-Japanese War.

December 1937 Japanese aircraft sink USS *Panay*.

December

December 7 Hawaii Some 183 Japanese aircraft attack the US Pacific Fleet at Pearl Harbor. They destroy 16 ships and 188 aircraft, damage or sink 10 other vessels, and kill 2,000 people.

December 8 United States The United States declares war on Japan.

December 8 Soviet Union Adolf Hitler halts the German advance on Moscow for the winter.

December 10 Pacific Ocean About 90 Japanese aircraft sink two British warships, *Prince of Wales* and *Repulse*, with the loss of 730 sailors.

The Kwantung Army

The Kwantung Army, also known as the Guandong Army, was originally a small garrison stationed in Manchuria, northern China, to defend Japan's commercial interests. In 1931, operating without government approval, the Japanese army's commanders faked a bombing on a train and occupied all of Manchuria. The army remained in northern China until the end of World War II, rising to a peak strength of around 700,000 men. It finally surrendered after the Soviet advance in August 1945.

Students undergo military training in the 1930s with guns that only fire blanks.

Many conservatives resented what they saw as Japan's humiliation. They argued Japan should look to traditional values, such as those followed by Japan's warriors, the samurai.

Hard-Liners Take Control

As militaristic views grew more popular, the Japanese army increasingly acted outside government control. It invaded Manchuria in northern China in 1931 (see box, left). The Japanese government itself became dominated by militarists. In July 1941, they ordered the invasion of Indochina, whose colonial government had fallen after Germany's defeat of France in 1940. In response, the United States, Britain, and the Dutch East Indies prohibited all exports to Japan.

Toward War

Japan had to import 80 percent of its oil, so it would soon run out. Its military planners decided to go to war to seize their own oil supplies. Their best chance lay in

Timeline
1942
January– February

January 5 Soviet Union Stalin's troops counterattack; their initial success halts as the Germans set up defenses.

January 20 Germany The "Final Solution"—the extermination of Europe's Jews—becomes key to Nazi war plans at the Wannsee Conference in Berlin.

January

KEY:

Pacific

Europe and North Africa

Eastern Front

January 10–11 Dutch East Indies Japanese troops attack the Dutch East Indies to capture the oil fields of the island chain.

January 13 Atlantic Ocean U-boats attack shipping off the US East Coast.

January 16–19 Germany Hitler sacks more than 30 senior generals who want to withdraw in the face of Soviet attacks on the Eastern Front.

← Chinese residents flee Nanking as the Japanese close in on the city in December 1937.

The Rape of Nanking

The Rape of Nanking took place during the Sino-Japanese War late in 1937. Japanese soldiers captured the old Chinese capital of Nanking (Nanjing) and began nearly two months of the rape, torture, and murder of civilians. The slaughter came to an end in February 1938. It was stopped as a result of international outrage—but also to prevent the spread of disease from the many corpses. In total, up to 200,000 Chinese were killed.

a rapid victory, which meant neutralizing the US Navy. The United States issued an ultimatum for Japan to withdraw from Indochina on November 26, 1941, but it had become irrelevant. On the same day, the Japanese fleet sailed from positions north of Japan bound for Pearl Harbor.

Japan's *Yamato* was one of the largest battleships in the world when it was built in 1937. ⇒

February 8 Singapore
Japanese troops land on the British-held island of Singapore.

February 27–29 Java Sea The Battle of the Java Sea. Japanese inflict heavy losses on an Allied fleet, sinking five cruisers and five destroyers to one Japanese cruiser lost.

February

February 11–12 North Sea The Channel Dash sees German battle cruisers speed to the North Sea before the British can stop them.

February 14 Singapore
The British at Singapore surrender after the Japanese cut the island's water supply.

Pearl Harbor

In US history, December 7, 1941, is the "day of infamy" when Japan launched a surprise attack on the United States. The attack changed the course of World War II.

Smoke billows from the USS *West Virginia* at Pearl Harbor. The ship sank, but was salvaged. →

Timeline
1942
March – April

March

March 9 Dutch East Indies Allied resistance ends in surrender; the Japanese gain possession of their "Southern Resources Area."

March 28–29 France British commandos attack the dry dock at St. Nazaire; 144 men are killed and many more are captured.

March 7 Burma British soldiers evacuate the capital, Rangoon, as the Japanese enter.

March 11 Philippines US general Douglas MacArthur is evacuated from the Philippines to Australia; he makes his famous promise, "I shall return."

KEY:

 Pacific

Europe and
North Africa

 Eastern
Front

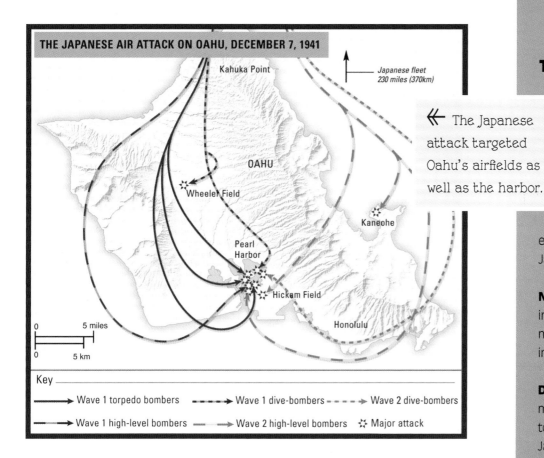

THE JAPANESE AIR ATTACK ON OAHU, DECEMBER 7, 1941

Kahuka Point

Japanese fleet
230 miles (370km)

OAHU

Wheeler Field

Kaneohe

The Japanese
attack targeted
Oahu's airfields as
well as the harbor.

Pearl
Harbor

Hickam Field

Honolulu

0   5 miles

0   5 km

Key

→ Wave 1 torpedo bombers   ---→ Wave 1 dive-bombers   ---→ Wave 2 dive-bombers

→ Wave 1 high-level bombers   ---→ Wave 2 high-level bombers   ✵ Major attack

As tension grew between the United States and Japan, in May 1940, President Franklin D. Roosevelt ordered the Pacific Fleet to Pearl Harbor, in Hawaii. It became the largest US naval base in the Pacific.

The Operation Begins

The Japanese planned an attack on Hawaii that would destroy the US Pacific Fleet. Six aircraft carriers and two battleships sailed from the Japanese Kurile Islands

Timeline

May 1940 Roosevelt sends the US Pacific Fleet to Pearl Harbor, Hawaii.

August 1, 1941 The United States and its allies impose an embargo on oil exports to Japan.

November 30, 1941 US intelligence decrypts Japanese messages anticipating an attack in the Pacific.

December 6, 1941 Roosevelt makes a final appeal for peace to Emperor Hirohito, but Japan's aircraft carriers are already steaming toward Hawaii.

December 7, 1941 Japanese aircraft attack Pearl Harbor and airfields on Oahu.

December 8, 1941 United States declares war on Japan.

December 11, 1941 Japan's allies, Germany and Italy, declare war on the United States.

April 9 Philippines US and Filipino forces in the Philippines surrender to the Japanese. Some 78,000 prisoners are forced to march 65 miles (105 km) into captivity; many die along the way.

April

April 18 Japan In a raid led by James Doolittle, 16 US B-25 bombers launched from an aircraft carrier attack Tokyo and other Japanese cities; the raid alarms Japan's leaders, who decide to seek a battle to destroy US naval power in the Pacific.

Isoroku Yamamoto (1884–1943)

Admiral Yamamoto, who planned the Pearl Harbor attack, was one of Japan's leading naval strategists. He believed that the attack would buy Japan time against an enemy that was industrially superior. He was later involved in the Battle of Midway, where Japan lost its naval supremacy. He died when his aircraft was shot down.

↑ A photo taken by a Japanese pilot shows the easy target the US warships offered.

for the Central Pacific on November 26, 1940. Keeping strict radio silence in order to avoid detection, the force reached a position 230 miles (370 km) north of Pearl Harbor.

An Easy Target

US Army intelligence was aware that a US base in Asia might be attacked—but not where. Warnings only reached Hawaii after the attack. The US forces at Pearl Harbor were therefore completely unready. They had even grouped their ships and aircraft together to make them easier to guard. This made them a sitting target for Japanese pilots.

Yamamoto was wary of going to war against an industrial superpower. »

Timeline
1942
May – June

May 8 Pacific Ocean In the Battle of the Coral Sea, the US Navy loses a carrier; the Japanese lose a smaller carrier, but a large number of aircraft.

May 31 Germany Britain launches its first "1,000 bomber raid" on Cologne, where 59,000 people are left homeless.

May

May 26–31 North Africa Rommel attacks the British Eighth Army in the Battle of Gazala.

KEY:

▮ Pacific

▮ Europe and North Africa

▮ Eastern Front

This diagram of Pearl Harbor shows the positions of the US vessels that were sunk or damaged. →

DAMAGE AT PEARL HARBOR

Pearl City
East Loch
Middle Loch
Battleship Row
PEARL HARBOR

0   1 mile
0   1 km

Key
— Sunk
— Badly damaged
— Damaged
— Undamaged

The Aerial Attack

At 7:48 A.M. on Sunday, December 7, 1941, the first of three waves of Japanese airplanes began attacking Pearl Harbor and nearby airfields. Soldiers, sailors, and marines reacted bravely but ineffectively. When the attackers departed at 10:00 A.M., they left more than 2,400 people dead, 188 US aircraft destroyed on the ground, and 16 ships sunk or damaged, including four sunken battleships.

The United States Declares War

Next day, Roosevelt addressed the US Congress and asked for a declaration of war against Japan. The Senate voted unanimously to declare war; in the House of Representatives, only Representative Jeannette Rankin of Montana voted against the conflict.

What Did Roosevelt Know?

Lasting controversy still surrounds how much Roosevelt knew about an attack on Pearl Harbor. Some historians think he ignored intelligence warnings because he wanted an excuse to take the United States into war. While there were rumors of a Japanese attack, however, it is likely that the president did not expect it to be on the US Pacific Fleet. US planners thought British or Dutch colonies in East and Southeast Asia were more obvious targets for a Japanese attack.

June 10–13 North Africa Rommel's way to Tobruk is open as British withdraw after the Battle of Gazala.

June 28 Soviet Union The Germans launch summer offensive, Operation Blue, into southern Russia to capture oil fields in the Caucasus.

June

June 4 Pacific Ocean The Battle of Midway. Japan's fleet aims to seize the US base at Midway Island and destroy the US Pacific Fleet. Despite having fewer ships, US forces win a decisive victory, sinking four Japanese carriers and destroying 332 aircraft.

June 21 North Africa Rommel captures Tobruk.

Japan's Asian Advance

Pearl Harbor was just the start of Japan's campaign of conquest in the Pacific. A rapid onslaught against Allied forces secured conquests across the region.

Japanese troops on a →
railroad locomotive
celebrate their rapid
conquest of Malaya.

Timeline
1942
July–
September

July 4–10 Soviet Union After a two-month siege, the Germans capture the port of Sevastopol and about 90,000 Red Army troops.

August 7 Guadalcanal US Marines land on Guadalcanal and face fierce Japanese resistance as they attempt to capture the airstrip at Henderson Field.

July

August

KEY:

Pacific

Europe and
North Africa

Eastern
Front

August 9 Pacific Ocean In a heavy defeat for the US Navy, the Japanese sink four US cruisers at the Battle of Savo Island.

↑ The Japanese used bicycles to advance rapidly on jungle roads.

Many Japanese officers knew there were great risks in a long war against the United States and Britain. They determined to capture territories that were rich in resources or strategically important as fast as possible.

The First Defeats

On December 8 (actually the same day as Pearl Harbor, but on the other side of the international date line), Japan invaded Thailand and northern Malaya. It also attacked the island of Hong Kong. By Christmas Day, the Japanese had captured the British colony.

← A British infantryman surrenders during the Japanese advance in Malaya.

Timeline

Deember 9, 1941 Thailand surrenders.

December 23, 1941 The Japanese capture Wake Island.

December 25, 1941 The British surrender Hong Kong.

January 11, 1942 The Japanese capture the Malay capital at Kuala Lumpur.

February 14, 1942 The British surrender Singapore: it is the British army's biggest single defeat.

March 8, 1942 The last of the islands of the Dutch East Indies surrenders.

May 26, 1942 The last Allied forces leave Burma.

August 23 Soviet Union A raid by 600 German bombers on Stalingrad kills thousands.

September 2 Poland The Nazis "clear" the Jewish Warsaw Ghetto; more than 50,000 Jews are killed.

September

August 19 France A combined Canadian, British, and US force attacks the port of Dieppe. It is a disaster, with most men killed.

Bushido: The Way of the Warrior

Bushido was the code of behavior followed by Japan's samurai warriors. It involved complete obedience to superiors, contempt for death and pain, and a mastery of military skills. Recruits were taught that death was preferable to surrender. That belief cost the Allies and Japanese heavy casualties during the Pacific War. It also underlay Japan's use of suicide tactics (kamikaze) toward the end of the war. Another Bushido principle was cruelty toward POWs and civilian populations.

Fighting the British

In Malaya, Japanese troops made rapid progress down through the mainland. Its capital, Kuala Lumpur, fell on January 11, 1942. By then, Japan had conquered two-thirds of the country.

Allied forces in Malaya retreated to Singapore, just off the tip of the Malay Peninsula. Although small, the island was a key British colony, which controlled vital sea routes. The British defenders outnumbered the attackers, but three days after the Japanese captured the island's reservoirs on February 12, the British surrendered.

The British surrender at Singapore, three days after the Japanese seize the reservoirs. ⇓

Timeline
1942
October–December

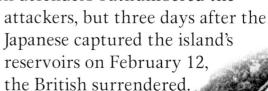

October 23 North Africa
The Second Battle of El Alamein begins in Egypt.

October ●━━━━━━━━━━━━━━━━━━━━━━━● November

November 2–4 North Africa
The Second Battle of El Alamein. Rommel is forced to retreat; it is the first major defeat suffered by German forces during the war.

KEY:

- ▢ Pacific
- ▢ Europe and North Africa
- ▢ Eastern Front

The Japanese drove the British from Burma back into India and the Chinese back into China. →

THE JAPANESE INVASION OF BURMA, 1941–1942

Imphal
INDIA
Lashio
CHINA
Mandalay
Salween River
BURMA
Yenangyaung
BAY OF BENGAL
Toungou
Sittang River
THAILAND
Rangoon
Moulmein
Bangkok

0   250 miles
0   400 km

Key
→   Japanese attacks, January–May 1942
─   Burma Road

Dutch East Indies

The naval Battle of the Java Sea on February 27, 1942, was a decisive victory for the Japanese. It effectively ended Allied resistance in the Dutch East Indies (now Indonesia). By March 8, all the islands of the group had surrendered.

Burma Falls

In Burma, meanwhile, the Japanese invaded in January 1942. Hampered by poor British decision making, Allied forces were forced to retreat toward the Indian border. By May, the Japanese were in charge of the whole country. In six months, the Japanese had achieved victories throughout Southeast Asia. The Dutch and British colonial empires were gone.

Jungle Warfare

The Japanese were masters of fighting in the dense, hot, and humid forests of Southeast Asia. Normal tactical maneuvers were impossible and heat exhaustion was common. The most serious problems were diseases like malaria. Fungus and bacteria thrived; the smallest cut could become infected.

← Indian troops in the British army advance through a Malay plantation.

November 19 Soviet Union General Georgi Zhukov launches an attack to relieve Stalingrad; the pincer movement traps the Germans in the city and the German front collapses.

December

December 19 Soviet Union A German counterattack fails to rescue the Sixth Army trapped in Stalingrad, where conditions are deteriorating and food is short.

Fall of the Philippines

The capture of the Philippines was a crucial part of Japan's strategy to secure an empire in the Southwest Pacific and to remove US power from the region.

US prisoners await their fate after being captured at Bataan. »

Timeline
1943
January–
March

January 10 Guadalcanal
Some 50,000 US troops attack the Japanese defenders, who are starving; many are also sick.

February 14–22 North Africa
Inexperienced US troops suffer heavy losses in the Battle of Kasserine Pass.

January

February

KEY:

 Pacific

 Europe and North Africa

Eastern Front

January 18 Poland
Jewish fighters in the Warsaw Ghetto begin attacking German troops.

January 31 Guadalcanal
US troops finally capture the island of Guadalcanal.

February 2 Soviet Union
The Siege of Stalingrad ends when 93,000 German troops surrender.

The Philippines—a group of some 7,000 islands— were of vital strategic importance. They had been a US colony since 1898. The US government planned to return them to Filipino rule, but growing Japanese power had isolated the islands. By mid-1941, the Philippines were threatened on three sides.

US Response

As diplomatic relations with Japan deteriorated, the United States reinforced the Philippines. In July 1941, General MacArthur was made head of a new command in the region, the US Army Forces in the Far East (USAFFE). MacArthur urged his superiors to adopt an ambitious program to build up the Philippines as a base of US power. With limited naval resources available, he asked for the creation of a huge air force in the islands.

Japanese troops land on the US-held island of Corregidor on ⭣ May 6, 1942.

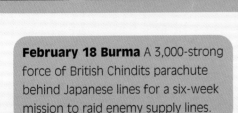

Timeline

July 1941 General Douglas MacArthur commands USAFFE.

December 10, 1941 Japanese troops land on Luzon, followed by more two days later.

December 19, 1941 Japanese troops land on Mindanao.

January 2, 1942 Japanese enter Manila, the capital.

January 9, 1942 Japanese attack US positions on the Bataan Peninsula.

January 22, 1942 US troops fall back.

March 12, 1942 MacArthur leaves for Australia.

April 10, 1942 The Bataan Death March begins.

May 6, 1942 Japanese troops land on Corregidor.

May 8, 1942 US forces surrender.

February 18 Burma A 3,000-strong force of British Chindits parachute behind Japanese lines for a six-week mission to raid enemy supply lines.

March 15 Soviet Union The Germans launch Operation Citadel, a plan to destroy Red Army troops near the city of Kursk.

March

February 16 Germany Students demonstrate against Hitler's regime in Munich; the leaders are executed.

March 2–5 Bismarck Sea In the Battle of the Bismarck Sea, Allied warships sink eight Japanese transports and four destroyers.

March 14 Soviet Union German forces destroy the Soviet Third Tank Army, forcing Soviets to abandon newly won territory on the Eastern Front.

Bataan Death March

The Japanese forced more than 72,000 American and Filipino prisoners to march with no food or water more than 65 miles (105 km) toward a camp. Weak, sick, and tired, any prisoners who fell back were executed. Some 18,000 men died. General Homma, who ordered the march, was executed after the war.

 US defense was concentrated around Manila Bay on the island of Luzon.

Japan Attacks

By December 1941, MacArthur's army and air force had grown. They were to prove ineffectual, however. When Japanese air raids began that month, more than half the US aircraft were destroyed in two days. The main Japanese landing followed on December 22; Japanese forces entered the capital, Manila, on January 2, 1942. On January 5, US and Filipino forces completed their withdrawal to Bataan, a mountainous peninsula covered in jungle on the island of Luzon. In their rapid withdrawal, the troops left behind most of their equipment. Troops were on half rations; within weeks, they were eating mules.

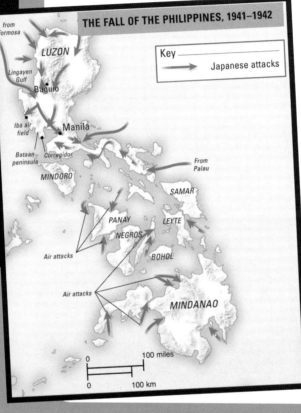

THE FALL OF THE PHILIPPINES, 1941–1942

from Formosa

LUZON

Lingayen Gulf

Baguio

Iba air field

Manila

Bataan peninsula Corregidor

MINDORO

From Palau

SAMAR

PANAY LEYTE

NEGROS

Air attacks

BOHOL

Air attacks

MINDANAO

Key
→ Japanese attacks

0   100 miles

0   100 km

Campaign for Bataan

Japanese forces were weakened after their advance. Their commander, General Homma, launched his first attack on Bataan on January 9. MacArthur remained confident that his troops could hold out.

Timeline
1943
April–
June

April 12 Soviet Union The Germans find a mass grave in Katyn Forest containing the bodies of 10,000 Polish army officers executed by the Soviet secret police in 1939.

April 17 Germany US bombers attack the German city of Bremen.

April

May

May 13 North Africa Axis forces surrender to the Allies; 620,000 Axis casualties and prisoners have been lost in the campaign.

KEY:

Pacific

Europe and North Africa

Eastern Front

By the end of February, however, the Bataan defenders were suffering from malnutrition, malaria, and dysentery. The US government, wanting a sign of US strength, forbade the troops to surrender but forced MacArthur to evacuate to Australia. Meanwhile, Homma launched a fresh attack on April 3. Exhausted, the defenders finally broke. US commander Jonathan Wainwright withdrew to the island of Corregidor to organize what few defenses remained in the Philippines. The forces left on Luzon surrendered on April 9.

For a month, the underground fortress on Corregidor was the site of the final US stand (see box, right). It fell on May 8, 1942.

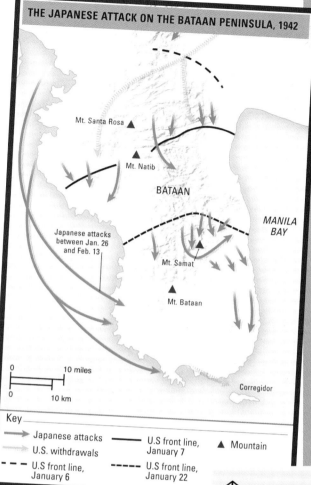

THE JAPANESE ATTACK ON THE BATAAN PENINSULA, 1942

Mt. Santa Rosa
Mt. Natib
BATAAN
MANILA BAY
Japanese attacks between Jan. 26 and Feb. 13
Mt. Samat
Mt. Bataan
Corregidor

0 10 miles
0 10 km

Key
Japanese attacks — U.S front line, January 7 ▲ Mountain
U.S. withdrawals
U.S front line, January 6 — U.S front line, January 22

⌃ Corregidor was the only escape from the jungle-covered, mountainous Bataan Peninsula.

Corregidor

As the Japanese advanced in May 1942, US forces fell back to the tiny fortified island of Corregidor 2 miles (3.2 km) east of the Bataan Peninsula. More than 11,000 men took shelter in its tunnels, but water and supplies began to run out. Facing a Japanese onslaught, the garrison surrendered. On May 8, US commander General Jonathan Wainwright ordered all remaining US and Filipino troops on the islands to surrender.

May 16–17 Germany The Dambusters Raid. The British use "bouncing bombs" to destroy dams in Germany's industrial Ruhr region.

June 10 Germany British and US bombers begin Operation Pointblank, a year-long series of attacks on German industry.

June

May 16 Poland The Warsaw Ghetto uprising ends; it has been harshly repressed by the Germans.

The Battle of the Coral Sea

By the spring of 1942, the rapid advances in Southeast
Asia and the Pacific created a split in priorities and almost
brought the Japanese to defeat in the Coral Sea.

A US Avenger bomber
launches its torpedo
during maneuvers. →→

Timeline

1943
July–
September

July 12–13 Soviet Union The
Soviets narrowly defeat the Germans
at Kursk. The battle leaves 500,000
casualties dead, injured, or missing.

July 25 Italy The king of Italy sacks
Benito Mussolini. The new leader, Pietro
Badoglio, hopes that the Allies will occupy
Italy before it falls under German control.

July   August

KEY:

- Pacific
- Europe and North Africa
- Eastern Front

July 5 Soviet Union The Battle
of Kursk is the largest tank battle
in history; the Germans make little
progress against the Soviets.

July 10 Sicily
Operation Husky: US
and British troops
invade the island.

July 24–August 2 Germany
The British bomb Hamburg,
killing around 50,000 civilians
and leaving 800,000 homeless.

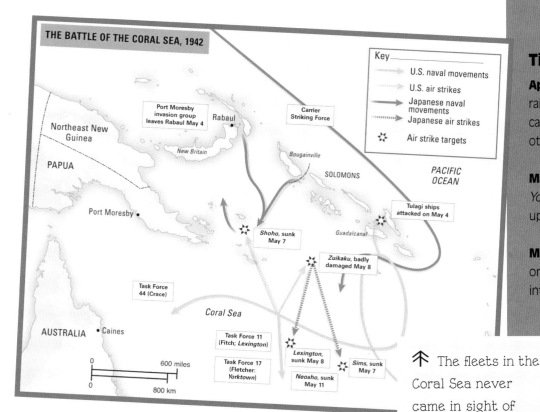

THE BATTLE OF THE CORAL SEA, 1942

Key
→ U.S. naval movements
⟶ U.S. air strikes
→ Japanese naval movements
⟶ Japanese air strikes
✧ Air strike targets

Port Moresby invasion group leaves Rabaul May 4
Rabaul
Carrier Striking Force
Northeast New Guinea
PAPUA
New Britain
Bougainville
SOLOMONS
PACIFIC OCEAN
Port Moresby •
Tulagi ships attacked on May 4
Shoho, sunk May 7
Guadalcanal
Zuikaku, badly damaged May 8
Task Force 44 (Crace)
Coral Sea
AUSTRALIA • Caines
Task Force 11 (Fitch; Lexington)
Task Force 17 (Fletcher; Yorktown)
Lexington, sunk May 8
Sims, sunk May 7
Neosho, sunk May 11
0   600 miles
0   800 km

⇧ The fleets in the Coral Sea never came in sight of one another.

Timeline

April 18, 1942 The Doolittle raid; US bombers from the carrier *Hornet* attack Tokyo and other cities.

May 1, 1942 US carriers *Yorktown* and *Lexington* meet up in Coral Sea.

May 3, 1942 Japanese landings on Tulagi confirm US intelligence to be correct.

May 4, 1942 US–Australian Task Force 44 joins US carriers in Coral Sea. *Yorktown* launches strikes against Tulagi invasion force.

May 7, 1942 Battle of the Coral Sea begins; Japanese sink the US destroyer *Sims*; the Japanese lose a light carrier.

May 8, 1942 Japanese *Zuikaku* loses almost all its aircraft, the *Shokaku* is hit three times. The *Yorktown* is hit and the *Lexington* sunk; the battle ends with no clear victor.

Since the attack on Pearl Harbor, the Japanese had enjoyed a string of victories. After their rapid successes, however, the Japanese were not sure what to do next.

They had planned Operation MO, an attack on Guadalcanal in the Solomon Islands, which guarded Allied convoy routes to Australia and New Zealand. Before the operation was fully put into action, however, a daring US attack changed Japanese intentions. The Doolittle raid was a reminder of the potential threat from aircraft based on US carriers (see box, page 24).

(see box, page 24).

August 17 Sicily The capture of Messina marks Allied victory on Sicily; from there, the Allies can attack the Italian peninsula.

September 25 Soviet Union. The Red Army recaptures Smolensk.

September

August 22–23 Soviet Union The Red Army recaptures Kharkov and threatens the Ukraine.

September 9 Italy US and British troops land in southern Italy.

September 12 Italy German airborne troops led by Lieutenant Colonel Otto Skorzeny rescue Mussolini from imprisonment in a hotel in the Italian mountains.

The Doolittle Raid

US strategists planned a carrier-based bomber raid on Japan itself. The raid, on April 18, 1942, was nicknamed Doolittle after its commander. Sixteen B-25 bombers were fitted with extra fuel tanks to increase their range. They bombed Tokyo before heading for China. The raid did little damage, but gave a major boost to US morale. It also scared Japan's leaders into seeking a battle with the US fleet—a battle they would lose.

One of the 16 B-25s leaves the carrier USS *Hornet* for Tokyo. ⇑

The Japanese decided to split their forces and continue with Operation MO while at the same time thrusting into the Central Pacific. By mid-April 1942, US intelligence believed that the Japanese would try to attack Port Moresby on New Guinea from their base at Rabaul on New Britain Island.

Battle of the Coral Sea

US admiral Chester Nimitz sent two aircraft carriers and their task forces to the Coral Sea to prevent the attack. The US carriers engaged a Japanese carrier force on May 7 in the first-ever naval battle in which the

A destroyer waits as the crew of the stricken *Lexington* abandon ship. ⇒

Timeline
1943
October–December

October

October 12–22 Italy Allied forces advance slowly north in bad weather toward German positions on the Gustav Line, in central Italy.

November

KEY:

Pacific

Europe and North Africa

Eastern Front

October 25 Burma The Burma to Siam (Thailand) rail link is completed. It has been built by the Japanese using Allied prisoners and local people as labor; about 12,000 prisoners have died from abuse, disease, and starvation.

November 6 Soviet Union The Soviets capture Kiev, trapping the German Seventeenth Army in the Crimea.

opposing fleets did not come into visual contact. The carriers launched all their aircraft, but neither found the enemy's main force. The sinking of the Japanese light carrier *Shoho* on the first day was the first Allied naval success of the Pacific war. On May 8, Japanese aircraft sank the USS *Lexington.* Japanese commanders believed their pilots had sunk both US carriers. However, a lack of air cover forced the Japanese to turn the invasion fleet back from Port Moresby and abandon their planned landings.

Students at a US Aeronautical Radio School take a class in deciphering Japanese codes. ⬇

Who Won the Battle?

The Battle of the Coral Sea was small, but it shaped future naval strategy. In the confusion, both sides claimed victory. The Japanese had lost a small carrier while destroying a large US carrier. The Americans had stopped the landings at Port Moresby, thereby ending Operation MO and protecting Australia. Most military historians judge the action a draw, but in spring 1942, US fortunes were so low that the result seemed like a major victory.

Cracking Japan's Codes

The ultimate Allied victory in World War II owed much to code breaking. By April 1942, US analysts had partially cracked the Japanese naval code, JN-25. The intelligence they learned gave them a decisive advantage. At the Battle of Midway in June 1942, for example, US carriers were waiting for the Japanese fleet. In April 1943, more intercepted signals allowed fighters to shoot down and kill the Japanese naval chief, Isoroku Yamamoto.

November 20 Gilbert Islands Some 18,600 US marines land on Tarawa and Bieto in the Gilbert Islands in the Pacific Ocean; more than 1,000 marines die before the islands are captured on 23rd.

December 26 Arctic Ocean The Battle of the North Cape sees British warships sink the German battleship *Scharnhorst.*

December

November 28 Iran British prime minister Winston Churchill meets President Roosevelt and Soviet leader Joseph Stalin in Tehran; they give priority to a cross-Channel invasion of occupied Europe in May 1944.

The Battle of Midway

Japan's thrust into the Central Pacific aimed to destroy the remaining US fleet. Instead, it was a disaster for the Imperial Japanese Navy.

The Japanese heavy cruiser *Mikuma* sinks after being damaged by US bombers. →→

Timeline
1944 January–February

January 14–17 Soviet Union Red Army attacks on the Germans besieging Leningrad force the Germans to retreat. Some 830,000 civilians have died in the three-year siege.

January 30 Marshall Islands Americans begin an attack on the Marshall Islands in the Pacific by landing on the undefended Majuro Atoll.

January

January 22 Italy Allied troops land at Anzio, behind the Gustav Line, and meet little resistance; but US general John Lucas orders his forces to dig in and create defensive positions.

KEY:

 Pacific

Europe and North Africa

 Eastern Front

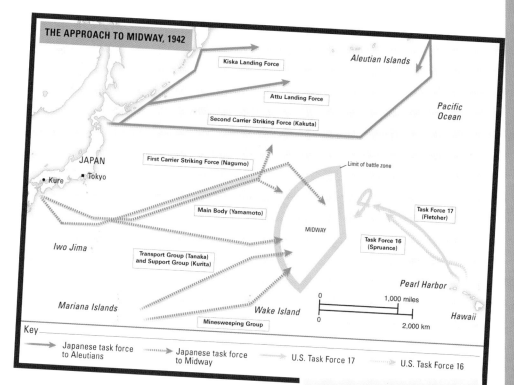

THE APPROACH TO MIDWAY, 1942

Kiska Landing Force

Aleutian Islands

Attu Landing Force

Pacific Ocean

Second Carrier Striking Force (Kakuta)

First Carrier Striking Force (Nagumo)

JAPAN

Kure Tokyo

Limit of battle zone

Task Force 17 (Fletcher)

Main Body (Yamamoto)

MIDWAY

Task Force 16 (Spruance)

Iwo Jima

Transport Group (Tanaka) and Support Group (Kurita)

Pearl Harbor

Mariana Islands

Wake Island

Minesweeping Group

Hawaii

0   1,000 miles
0   2,000 km

Key

→ Japanese task force to Aleutians
···→ Japanese task force to Midway
→ U.S. Task Force 17
···→ U.S. Task Force 16

⬆ Japan made thrusts to the Aleutian Islands and into the Central Pacific.

After Japan's thrust to isolate Australia was halted at the Battle of the Coral Sea, Japan's naval planners focused on defeating US carrier forces. They would occupy the Aleutian Islands off Alaska and seize Midway Island, an Allied airbase in the Central Pacific, to draw the US carriers into an unequal battle.

The Japanese fleet had more operational aircraft carriers and more experienced pilots flying superior Zero fighters. However, unknown to Japanese commander Isoroku Yamamoto, US intelligence had

Timeline

May 1942 The largest Japanese fleet ever assembled sails for the Central Pacific.

June 3, 1942 Japanese Northern Area Force occupies Kiska and Attu in the Aleutian Islands, but the Americans ignore the decoy. US bombers attack Japanese fleet at Midway, but cause little damage.

June 4, 1942 Japanese bombers score early successes at Midway.

June 4, 1942, 10:28 A.M. Bombers from USS *Enterprise* disable two Japanese carriers; the successes change the course of the war in the Pacific.

June 6, 1942 Americans sink Japanese heavy cruiser.

June 7, 1942 *Yorktown* is sunk by a Japanese submarine in the last engagement of the Battle of Midway.

February 4–24 Burma The Japanese launch Operation Ha-Go to drive the Allies back to the border with India.

February

February 1–4 Marshall Islands Some 40,000 US troops launch an amphibious assault against Kwajalein Atoll; they lose 1,000 men, against more than 11,600 Japanese dead.

February 18–22 Marshall Islands US forces seize Eniwetok Atoll, completing the conquest of the islands.

The Japanese Plan

In spring 1942, Isoroku Yamamoto sought to press home Japan's advantage in the Pacific. He gathered four large naval task forces. Three headed into the Central Pacific. The other struck north for the Aleutian Islands, off Alaska, to draw off US forces. An amphibious force would attack Midway. The island was beyond US air cover, so the Americans would send their fleet to protect it. Yamamoto planned to combine his fleets into an overwhelming force and destroy the US Navy.

↑ US Devastator torpedo bombers are readied on the deck of the USS *Enterprise*.

cracked Japanese navy codes. US commanders therefore knew exactly what Yamamoto was planning. They got their carriers in place before the Japanese arrived, giving them the advantage of surprise. In addition, the Japanese thought they faced only two enemy aircraft carriers: in fact, they faced three, as *Yorktown* had survived the Battle of the Coral Sea and been repaired in only three days.

Nagumo's Error

On June 3, the Japanese seized remote islands in the Aleutians. The Americans stayed close to Midway, however, where a Japanese landing fleet was spotted the same day. Next day, Japanese aircaft gained such an

Timeline
1944
March–
April

March

March 7–8 India/Burma Operation U-Go begins; the Japanese assault aims to drive the Allies back into India by attacking their bases at Imphal and Kohima.

March 24 Burma Orde Wingate, commander of the Allied Chindits, dies in a plane crash.

March 20–22 Italy Allied attacks fail to overcome Monte Cassino, part of the Gustav Line.

March 29 India Japanese forces cut the road between the British bases at Imphal and Kohima, and begin the siege of Kohima.

KEY:

Pacific

Europe and
North Africa

Eastern
Front

← A Japanese fighter falls from the sky after being hit by US fire.

advantage in early clashes that fleet commander Chuichi Nagumo ordered a new wave of air strikes. He believed that he had driven off the US defenders—but he was mistaken.

US dive bombers surprised the Japanese fleet at 10:28 A.M. They destroyed the *Akagi* and *Kaga* and also hit the *Soryu* and *Hiryu*, which later sank. A Japanese attack destroyed the *Yorktown*, but that success had a high cost. The Japanese had lost four aircraft carriers, 332 aircraft, and hundreds of skilled pilots.

The Outcome

The Battle of Midway turned the tide in the Pacific theater the Japanese had dominated for six months. Their failure left them with a seriously weakened force.

The Zero

The Mitsubishi A6M Zero-Sen was the first carrier fighter capable of surpassing land-based aircraft. The Zero was deadly in a dogfight and could outmaneuver enemy fighters. With a top speed of 350 mph (560 km/h), the Zero was the basis of Japanese carrier aviation in the Battle of the Coral Sea and at Midway. More Zeros were made than any other wartime Japanese aircraft: 10,938 in total.

← The Japanese flag flies on US sovereign territory in the Aleutians.

April

April 4–13 India After Japanese attempts to break the Allied defense line fail, British forces attack the Japanese and begin to drive them back from Imphal and Kohima.

April 22 New Guinea An Allied invasion force commanded by US general Douglas MacArthur lands in Hollandia as part of Operation Cartwheel, which aims to drive the Japanese from northwestern New Guinea.

April 6–11 Burma Japanese attacks force the Chindits to evacuate their fortified position at "White City."

Island Hopping

By the start of 1944, US forces began an advance toward Japan. Their goal remained thousands of miles away, however, protected by the vast Pacific Ocean.

A US B-25 bombs Japanese positions in the Marshall Islands.

Timeline

1944
May–
June

May

May 9 Soviet Union The Red Army liberates the Black Sea port of Sevastopol.

May 11–18 Italy The Allies break through the Gustav Line near Monte Cassino.

May 18 Pacific Ocean US forces clear the Admiralty Islands of Japanese, effectively isolating the Japanese bases at Rabaul and Kavieng in the Southwest Pacific.

KEY:

Pacific

Europe and North Africa

Eastern Front

The strategic position in the → Pacific in mid-1944.

By 1944, the United States was ready to make two simultaneous thrusts: one into the Central Pacific, the other into the Southwest Pacific. US Navy admiral Chester Nimitz led the first, toward Japan itself, while US Army general Douglas MacArthur led the second. His aim was to neutralize Rabaul, the key Japanese base on New Guinea.

THE PACIFIC WAR, MID-1944

MANCHURIA · CHINA · KOREA · JAPAN · TIBET · BURMA · FORMOSA · THAILAND · FRENCH INDO-CHINA · PHILIPPINES · MALAYA · SUMATRA · BORNEO · NEW GUINEA · AUSTRALIA · PACIFIC OCEAN · Aleutian Islands · Wake Island · Mariana Islands · Guam · Marshall Islands · Caroline Islands · Gilbert Islands · Solomon Islands

0 1,500 miles / 0 1,500 km

Key — U.S. attacks late 1943–mid-1944 | Japanese control | Limit of Japanese control

Timeline

October 1943 US air campaign begins against Rabaul, New Guinea.

November 1943 United States retakes Solomon Islands and Tarawa.

February 7, 1944 United States captures Marshall Islands.

June 19–21, 1944 Battle of the Philippine Sea; Japan loses its naval aviation arm.

July 13, 1944 US forces capture Saipan, Marianas.

July 30, 1944 US forces secure north coast of New Guinea.

August 2, 1944 Tinian is taken.

August 10, 1944 Guam is taken.

← An Allied bomber attacks vessels in the harbor at Rabaul, one of many attacks on the port.

June 6 Northern France D-Day. The Allied invasion of Normandy, Operation Overlord, begins with paratroopers landing to seize key targets and amphibious landings on five beaches. By the end of the day, the Allies have a beachhead in Europe at the cost of 2,500 dead.

June 22 Soviet Union With huge numerical superiority, the Red Army launches Operation Bagration against German Army Group Center.

June

June 3 Italy German troops abandon Rome, which is occupied by US troops on June 5.

June 19–21 Philippine Sea The "Great Marianas Turkey Shoot." The Japanese lose three aircraft carriers and 346 combat aircraft in the Battle of the Philippine Sea.

June 30 Britain To date, 2,000 V1 "flying bombs" have been launched against British targets, mostly London.

Battle of Tarawa

Tarawa, fought between November 20 and 23, 1943, was the first US offensive in the Central Pacific. It was also the first time a US amphibious landing faced serious Japanese opposition. The attackers lost 1,500 out of 5,000 men on the first morning. Despite the chaos, the United States secured the island early on November 23. Fewer than one hundred of the island's 4,500 defenders surrendered. The losses shocked US commanders and the public at home.

US aircraft fly a raid against the Marianas in June 1940. ⤒

The Central Pacific

Nimitz's advance aimed to use amphibious landings to capture islands. It would establish bases and airfields that would eventually bring US forces within striking distance of Japan. Unlike MacArthur, whose landings often had the benefit of surprise, Nimitz' amphibious landings often took place under heavy fire. The small islands of the Central Pacific were far apart, so attackers could be easily spotted and surprise was harder to achieve.

Heavy Toll for Japan

The first thrust of Nimitz's advance secured the Marshall Islands. US commanders then targeted the Marianas, where marines landed on Saipan on June 15. It took a month of heavy fighting to win the island; some 29,000 Japanese soldiers and 22,000 civilians died. Marines went on to capture Tinian and Guam.

Timeline
1944
July–
August

July

July 7 Saipan Japanese forces launch a mass charge that breaks US lines before it stalls and fails.

July 20 Germany German officers try to kill Hitler. Count Schenk von Stauffenberg plants a bomb in a conference room, but fails to kill Hitler. The failure leads to the execution of dozens of suspects.

July 9 Saipan US troops secure the island; at least 8,000 Japanese troops and civilians have committed suicide rather than surrender.

July 21 Guam US troops begin landing on Guam, the largest of the Mariana Islands.

KEY:

Pacific

Europe and North Africa

Eastern Front

Japan sent its Mobile Fleet to defend the islands. It met the US Fifth Fleet in the Philippine Sea. The battle that followed ended in disaster for the Japanese, who lost 346 aircraft to just 30 US planes. The Battle of the Philippine Sea was the largest carrier action of the Pacific War. It was so one-sided the US pilots nicknamed it the "Great Marianas Turkey Shoot."

The loss of the Marianas and the devastation of the Mobile Fleet were disastrous for Japan. The enemy had breached its ring of defensive islands and exposed Japan to attack.

US Submarine Campaign

When the war in the Pacific began, the US submarine fleet was small and largely obsolete. It expanded rapidly and was vital in cutting Japan's movement of supplies. New, more modern submarines were introduced like the well-armed Tench class with a range of some 11,000 nautical miles (20,370 km). In 1944, US submarines sank over half of the 3.3 million tons of merchant shipping lost by Japan. By 1945, Japan's merchant fleet was finished— and Japan's supply routes were destroyed.

US troops evacuate Japanese civilians on Saipan. Many Japanese killed themselves rather than surrender. ⬇

August 1 Poland The Warsaw Uprising—38,000 soldiers of the Polish Home Army fight the Germans.

August 25 France General Dietrich von Choltitz, commander of the German garrison in Paris, surrenders the city to the Allies.

August

August 10 Marianas Islands Japanese resistance on Guam finally ends after fierce fighting; however, the last Japanese soldier on the island does not give himself up until 1960.

The Battle of Leyte Gulf

The October 1944 naval battle around the Philippine Islands—the largest naval battle of World War II—sealed the fate of the wartime Imperial Japanese Navy.

Corsairs armed with 500-pound (227 kg) bombs prepare to take off from a Central Pacific base. →→

Timeline
1944
September–
October

September

September 2 Finland
Finland accepts a peace treaty with the Soviet Union and severs relations with Germany.

September 17 Holland Operation Market Garden. The Allies suffer heavy losses as paratroopers try to seize key bridges.

September 22–25 Holland
Paratroopers retreat from Arnhem.

KEY:

 Pacific

Europe and
North Africa

 Eastern
Front

A kamikaze attacks ↑
the USS *Columbia* in
January 1945, during
US landings in the
Philippines.

T he capture of the Marshall
and the Mariana Islands
brought US forces to a position
from which they could assault the Philippines. The first
objective of General Douglas MacArthur was Leyte, an
island in the southern Philippines. An amphibious
assault would be supported by two naval fleets.

The Japanese plan to defend the islands was complex.
A decoy force would draw the US vessels away, while
two attack forces would head for Leyte from the west

Timeline

October 20, 1944 US forces
land on eastern Leyte, in the
Philippines.

October 22, 1944 Japan's
decoy force and First Attack
Force head for the Philippines.

October 23, 1944 US
submarines sink two Japanese
cruisers and severely damage a
third.

October 24, 1944 Nearly 300
US aircraft attack Kurita's force;
Kurita withdraws to ambush
US carriers.

October 25, 1944 Japan's
Force C all but destroyed. Force
A threatens vulnerable US
landing fleet.

October 26, 1944 After a
battle lasting 2 hours and 23
minutes, US vessels defeat a
larger Japanese force at Leyte
Gulf.

November 1944 Japanese
launch offensive on Leyte.

(continued)

October 2 Poland After a two-
month battle, the last Poles in
Warsaw surrender to the Germans;
150,000 Poles have died.

October 20 Philippines The US Sixth Army lands
on Leyte Island in the Philippines; as he wades
ashore, US general Douglas MacArthur keeps a
promise he made two years earlier: "I shall return."

October

October 23–26 Philippines The Japanese
Combined Fleet is defeated heavily at the Battle of
Leyte Gulf. It loses 500 aircraft, 28 ships, and a
submarine; US losses are 200 aircraft and six ships.

Timeline (continued)

December 7, 1944 More US troops land on Leyte.

December 15, 1944 US troops land on Mindoro Island, southwest of Luzon.

January 9, 1945 US Sixth Army lands at Lingayen Gulf in western Luzon.

March 3, 1945 Manila captured by US troops after a month of fighting; the city is largely destroyed and 100,000 are dead.

April 17, 1945 US landings on Mindanao, the largest island in southern Philippines.

May 3, 1945 US forces take the port of Davao with no resistance.

End June 1945 US forces now control most of coast.

June 30, 1945 Despite pockets of Japanese resistance, Mindanao is in US control.

THE BATTLE OF LEYTE GULF, 1944

Key
→ Japanese fleet movements
⟶ Japanese air strikes
→ U.S. fleet movements
⟶ U.S. air strikes
⬭ Position of U.S. carrier task groups, 0600, October 24

Ozawa's Third Fleet, Second Attack Force, LUZON, Manila, MINDORO, San Bernardino Strait, U.S. Third Fleet, Sibuyan Sea, SAMAR, PANAY, LEYTE, NEGROS, U.S. Seventh Fleet, First Attack Force (Kurita), PALAWAN, Southern Force (Nishimura), MINDANAO, 200 miles, 300 km, BRITISH NORTH BORNEO, Brunei

↑ The battle began the US reconquest of the Philippines.

and south. The plan would risk nearly the whole Japanese navy.

Battle Begins

On October 23, 1944, US submarines spotted the Japanese attack force and sank two cruisers. A Japanese raid on the US Third Fleet sank the carrier *Princeton*. On October 24, US aircraft sank the carrier *Musashi* and damaged the *Yamato*. The Japanese commander Takeo Kurita appeared to retreat.

Taking the Bait

Meanwhile, the US Third Fleet had followed Japan's decoy force, leaving the Leyte landings exposed. Kurita turned around in the darkness and headed back toward Leyte. Japan's Force C and Second Attack Force were approaching through the Surigao Strait. The US Seventh Fleet was vulnerable to a pincer movement. As Force C sailed down the strait, however, it was attacked by US Task Group 77. The southern pincer collapsed.

Timeline
1944 November– December

November

November 7 Japan The Japanese hang the spy Richard Sorge, a German newspaper correspondent who has been passing Japanese and German secrets to the Soviet Union.

November 11–12 Iwo Jima US warships bombard the Japanese-held island for the first time.

November 24 Japan US B-29 Superfortresses flying from the Mariana Islands raid Tokyo for the first time.

KEY:

Pacific
Europe and North Africa

Eastern Front

Kurita Withdraws

Kurita now moved against the weak US landing fleet.
Although he had a huge advantage in numbers of ships,
however, his fuel was running low and he was anxious
that US backup might arrive. His battered force had
had enough. He turned around and left Leyte.

A New Tactic

Leyte Gulf was a great US victory. The crippling
defeat marked the virtual end of Japan's Pacific threat.
It also marked the first major use of kamikaze attacks.
This tactic would become more
common as the conflict went on.

October 1944. Led by the
Nagato, Kurita's First
Attack Force steams
⬇ toward the Philippines.

Kamikaze

Meaning "divine
wind," kamikaze were
suicide pilots of the
Japanese air force
who flew their bomb-
laden aircraft into
US ships. Japanese
vice admiral Onishi
said suicide missions
were ideal for novice
pilots: they just had
to fly into the target.
It was hard for US
antiaircraft gunners
to destroy kamikaze
planes in the air.
Mass raids began
over the Philippines
in October 1944,
reaching a peak off
Okinawa between
March and June 1945,
when 1,475 suicide
planes targeted US
ships in 10 separate
attacks.

December 16 Belgium Hitler begins Operation
Watch on the Rhine, which aims to capture
Antwerp. The Germans advance in thick fog. They
are stopped by US paratroopers in Bastogne.

December 4 Burma The British
Fourteenth Army begins the destruction
of Japanese forces in Burma.

December

December 5–7 Philippines
US forces begin their final
offensive against Japanese
lines on Leyte.

December 15 Philippines
The US 24th Division lands on
the island of Mindoro.

Iwo Jima and Okinawa

By the end of 1944, US forces were close to attacking Japan itself. They took part in two battles that would be among the hardest and most costly of the Pacific War.

US troops unload supplies at Iwo Jima. Everything was shipped in, even fresh water. →

Timeline
1945
January–February

January

January 12–17 Poland The Red Army begins its Vistula-Oder Offensive: two million men advance rapidly across the whole front.

January 30 Germany Soviet forces reach the Oder River, only 100 miles (160 km) from Berlin.

January 9 Philippines Units of the US Sixth Army make unopposed landings on the island of Luzon.

January 27 Poland The Red Army liberates the Nazi death camp at Auschwitz.

January 28 Belgium The German Ardennes Offensive has cost about 100,000 German lives, with about 81,000 US casualties.

KEY:

- Pacific
- Europe and North Africa
- Eastern Front

The final drive that would bring US forces within range of the Japanese home islands depended on the capture of two islands: Iwo Jima and Okinawa.

Iwo Jima

The volcanic island of Iwo Jima was a natural fortress defended by 21,000 Japanese. Major General Kuribayashi had built a defensive complex with miles of tunnels and trenches. He intended that his troops would take cover and lure US troops inland.

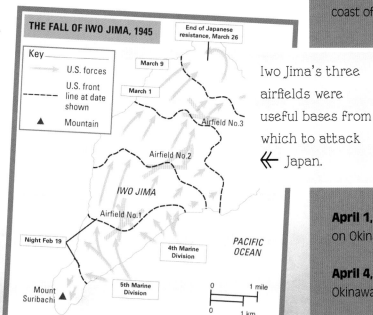

THE FALL OF IWO JIMA, 1945

End of Japanese resistance, March 26

Key
- U.S. forces
- U.S. front line at date shown
- ▲ Mountain

March 9

March 1

Airfield No.3

Airfield No.2

IWO JIMA

Airfield No.1

Night Feb 19

Mount Suribachi ▲

4th Marine Division

5th Marine Division

PACIFIC OCEAN

0 — 1 mile
0 — 1 km

Iwo Jima's three airfields were useful bases from which to attack ← Japan.

Timeline

February 17, 1945 US marines land on southwest coast of Iwo Jima.

February 23, 1945 US forces reach summit of Mt. Suribachi.

March 16, 1945 Iwo Jima declared secure.

April 1, 1945 US troops land on Okinawa.

April 4, 1945 US troops on Okinawa reach Machinato Line.

April 28, 1945 US forces reach second defensive line.

June 22, 1945 US troops finally take Okinawa.

← In the shadow of Mt. Suribachi, US marines take cover on a beach of black volcanic sand on Iwo Jima, March 5, 1945.

February 3 Philippines US forces enter Manila, capital of the Philippines; Japanese forces virtually destroy the city in a month's fighting known as the "Rape of Manila."

February 14 Germany As the Red Army advances, half of the 2.3 million population of German East Prussia flees west. Thousands die from cold or exhaustion.

February

February 4 Soviet Union Stalin, Roosevelt, and Churchill meet at Yalta to decide the division of postwar Europe.

February 13–14 Germany British bombers bomb Dresden, creating a firestorm that kills at least 50,000 people.

February 17 Iwo Jima US marines land on the island of Iwo Jima, which they capture after a month of heavy fighting.

Burma and China

The Japanese had driven the Allies from Burma in May 1942, but it remained strategically important. During 1944, the "forgotten army" of British and Indian troops began a jungle war that eventually ended the Japanese occupation. Meanwhile, fighting in China continued as Japanese troops captured Allied airfields. A reformed and reequipped Chinese army fought back successfully against Japanese attacks in March and April 1945. On May 9, Japanese troops were ordered out of southern China.

A warship fires rockets as a US landing craft approaches Okinawa. ⇒

The US Invasion

Preparations for Operation Detachment began in June 1944, when US bombers attacked Iwo Jima. Beginning on December 8, US forces bombed Iwo Jima every day for 72 days in the longest aerial bombing of the Pacific War. Two divisions of US marines landed on the beaches of Iwo Jima on February 17. The island was declared secure after nearly four weeks of fighting that took a high toll on both sides. Of the Japanese defenders, nearly 20,000 died.

The Battle for Okinawa

The next US target was Okinawa in the Ryukyu group of islands, between Kyushu, the most southerly of Japan's home islands, and Formosa (Taiwan). US and British carrier aircraft attacked airfields on Kyushu and

Timeline
1945
March–April

March

KEY:

Pacific

Europe and North Africa

Eastern Front

March 7 Japan A US bombing raid on Tokyo kills 83,000 people and destroys a large area of the Japanese capital.

March 16 Iwo Jima The Americans declare the island secure. They have lost 6,821 soldiers and sailors; of the 21,000 Japanese defenders, nearly 20,000 are dead.

March 23 Germany British and US forces start to cross the Rhine River. German troops offer little resistance.

Japanese prisoners → wait to be questioned on Okinawa on June 21.

Formosa to isolate Okinawa from March 1944. In the last week of March, Okinawa itself came under heavy naval bombardment and air attack.

The landings began on April 1, with some 182,000 US troops supported by an armada of warships. At sea, Japanese kamikaze pilots flew some 2,000 sorties, sinking 21 warships. It took until June 22 to declare Okinawa secure. Some 100,000 Japanese defenders died, along with about 12,000 Americans.

Okinawa had higher Allied casualties than any other Pacific War campaign. The losses made US planners fearful of the casualties that would result from an invasion of Japan itself.

US Marine Corps

The marines who led the Iwo Jima and Okinawa landings were amphibious soldiers of the US Navy. During the war, the Marine Corps suffered heavy losses because they were involved in the fiercest fighting.

Admiral Chester Nimitz wrote, "Among the Americans who served on Iwo Jima, uncommon valor was a common virtue."

THE FALL OF OKINAWA, 1945

Key
- → U.S. attacks
- → Japanese counterattacks
- Occupied by U.S. army, April 19
- — U.S. front line
- ······· Japanese defense line

Hedo • April 13
Bise
April 12
Taira
Nago
April 8
Onna
April 4
OKINAWA
Pacific Ocean
Machinato Line • Kuba
June 4 • Naha — April 4
Shuri
Shuri Line
June 21 • Kiyamu

0   20 miles
0   30 km

← Map of the fighting on Okinawa. US troops faced stiff resistance from the Japanese.

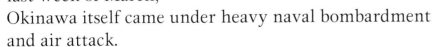

April 1 Okinawa Some 183,000 men of the US Tenth Army land on the island, which is only 325 miles (520 km) from Japan.

April 12 United States President Roosevelt dies of a brain hemorrhage; Vice President Harry S. Truman takes over as president.

April 28 Italy Mussolini is shot dead by partisans as he tries to flee to Austria.

April

April 7 Pacific Ocean US bombers on their way to Okinawa sink the *Yamato*, the world's largest battleship.

April 16 Germany The Soviets attack Berlin; they vastly outnumber the Germans in troops, tanks, weapons, and aircraft.

April 29 Italy German forces in Italy surrender to the Allies.

April 30 Germany Hitler and Eva Braun commit suicide in their bunker in Berlin.

The Surrender of Japan

As their forces neared Japan, US military planners faced a dilemma. Any invasion would likely cause huge casualties, among both troops and civilians.

Months after the blast, Hiroshima lies in ruins; about 4.5 square miles (11.65 sq km) of the city was flattened. →

Timeline
1945
May–
June

May

May 3 Burma Burma surrenders to the Allies without a fight after 38 months of Japanese occupation.

May 2 Germany The Reichstag falls to the Red Army after a savage three-day battle.

May 8 Europe Victory in Europe (VE) Day; the Allies formally accept the German surrender.

KEY:

 Pacific

Europe and North Africa

 Eastern Front

↑ Fires blazing in Takamatsu port silhouette bombs dropped from a B-29 flying at high altitude.

Timeline

July 16, 1945 The US Project Manhattan successfully tests the world's first atomic bomb at Alamogordo, New Mexico.

August 6, 1945 United States drops an atomic bomb on Hiroshima, Japan.

August 8, 1945 Soviet Union declares war on Japan.

August 9, 1945 United States drops a second atomic bomb on Nagasaki; the Soviet Red Army invades Manchuria to fight the Japanese Imperial Army.

August 10, 1945 Emperor Hirohito and Foreign Minister Shigenori Togo convince the Japanese military to accept defeat.

August 15, 1945 A cease-fire comes into effect.

September 2, 1945 Japan signs the formal surrender on the battleship USS *Missouri* in Tokyo Bay.

Both the United States and Japan were planning for a US invasion of Japan. Based on Japanese resistance elsewhere in the Pacific, US commanders feared that the invasion would be the most bloody of the war.

Japan's Defensive Preparations

In April 1945, the Japanese launched Operation Ketsu-go for two million soldiers to defend the four home islands and Korea. They increased their ground forces with the People's Volunteer Combat Corps, a home guard organization. Propaganda called for the country's defenders to fight to the end rather than endure the humiliation of living under US occupation.

June 22 Okinawa Japanese resistance ends on the island of Okinawa; the battle has cost the Japanese 100,000 dead, including some 26,000 civilians, many of whom choose to commit suicide.

June

June 1 Burma British troops are mopping up the 700,000 Japanese left scattered widely around Burma.

The Tokyo Fire Raids

The first great incendiary raid on Tokyo was on the night of March 9–10, 1945, when 279 B-29s dropped 2,000 tons of bombs. The resulting fires destroyed 25 percent of Tokyo's buildings, killed 83,000 people, injured 41,000, and left one million homeless. The B-29s returned twice more. Just three raids destroyed more than half the city, or some 50 square miles (129 sq km).

↑ Dust sucked in by the blast at ground level forms a mushroom cloud above Nagasaki.

"Little Boy," the atomic bomb used at Hiroshima, had the power of 15,000 tons of conventional explosives. ⇒

Bombing Campaign

In early 1945, US bombers began dropping incendiary bombs to start fires. The first raid used the new tactic on the night of March 9–10, 1945, on Tokyo. It devastated the city. After the capture of airfields on Iwo Jima, bombers expanded their operations to include daylight raids with high-explosive bombs. By May, US fighters had air superiority above Japan. Bombers flattened much of Japan's six major industrial centers: Kawasaki, Kobe, Nagoya, Osaka, Tokyo, and Yokahama.

Japanese Morale

The morale of Japanese civilians began to crumble as food and shelter grew scarce, and the infrastructure collapsed. Emperor Hirohito wanted to surrender, but the military refused.

Timeline

1945
July–
September

July 17–August 2 Germany US president Harry S. Truman, Stalin, and new British prime minister Clement Attlee meet at Potsdam to discuss postwar policy in Europe.

August 9 Manchuria A huge Soviet offensive begins against the Japanese Kwantung Army.

July

August

KEY:

- Pacific
- Europe and North Africa
- Eastern Front

August 6 Japan A B-29 Superfortress drops an atomic bomb on the Japanese city of Hiroshima, killing 70,000 and injuring a similar number.

August 9 Japan An atomic bomb is dropped on Nagasaki, killing 35,000 people. The Japanese decide to surrender.

A New Weapon

Meanwhile, after years of secret research, the United States had tested the first atomic bomb. The new president, Harry S. Truman, decided to use it against Japan rather than risk an invasion. The first atomic bomb was dropped on August 6 on Hiroshima, a city of 245,000 people. Two-thirds of the city was destroyed. When no Japanese surrender came, a second bomb was dropped on Nagasaki on August 9. Meanwhile, the Soviet Red Army attacked Japanese troops in China.

The Japanese Surrender

The Japanese military was forced to accept defeat. On August 15, a cease-fire came into effect. Hirohito spoke on the radio to tell the Japanese that they must "bear the unbearable." The war in the Pacific was over.

Emperor Hirohito's Broadcast

At noon on August 15, 1945, Emperor Hirohito made a radio broadcast. He told his people that it was his and their painful duty to surrender without further bloodshed. Hirohito had godlike status in Japan. He had never spoken directly to his people, many of whom had never heard his voice. His speech helped the transition from war to peace go more smoothly than some observers feared.

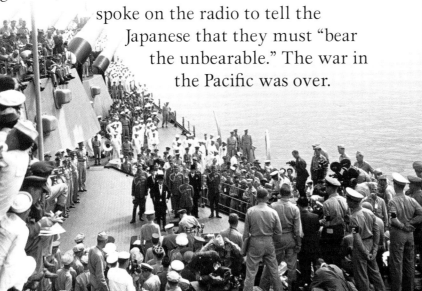

← Crew on the USS *Missouri* watch the formal Japanese surrender on September 2, 1945.

August 23 Manchuria The Soviet campaign against the Japanese ends in total victory.

September 2 Japan Aboard the US battleship *Missouri* in Tokyo Bay, Japanese officials sign the Instrument of Surrender; World War II is finally over.

September

August 15 Japan Victory over Japan (VJ) Day; the Japanese surrender is announced.

Glossary

amphibious assaults an attack by soldiers who land from the sea.

atoll a coral island of a reef surrounding a lagoon

atomic bomb an explosive device that creates huge power by splitting or fusing atoms

battleship the largest and most heavily armored type of warship

convoy a number of ships or vehicles traveling together

corps a military unit made up of several divisions

counterattack an attack by a defending force

decoy something used to lure the enemy into a trap

evacuation the removal of people from a dangerous area

garrison a military post

incendiary a bomb that is designed to start fires

infrastructure the roads, railroads, supplies, and organization that allow a community to function

intelligence information learned from secret services or code breakers

kamikaze a Japanese suicide pilot

marine a soldier based on a ship who fights on land

morale the emotional well-being of people

neutralize to make sure that an enemy force has no effect on the conflict

occupation military control of part of a country by forces from another

peninsula an area of land that juts into water

retaliation revenge for a previous event

strait a short, narrow stretch of water between two bodies of land

strategic useful in achieving a long-term goal

strategy a long-term plan of action

surrender to stop fighting and give in to the enemy

Further Reading

Books

Adams, Simon. *World War II (Eyewitness Books)*. Dorling Kindersley Children, 2007.

Brinkley, Douglas. *World War II Desk Reference*. Castle Books, 2008.

Cross, Robin. *World War II*. DK Publishing, 2007.

Davison, John. *Pacific War Day by Day*. MBI Publishing Co., 2006.

Dickson, Keith D. *World War II for Dummies*. For Dummies, 2001.

Doeden, Matt. *Weapons of World War II*. Capstone Press, 2008.

Grant, Reg. *World War II (DK Readers)*. DK CHILDREN, 2008.

Harris, Nathaniel. *World War II: Timelines*. Arcturus Publishing, 2007.

Horner, David. *World War II: The Pacific (Essential Histories)*. Rosen Publishing Group, 2010.

Hynson, Colin. *World War II: A Primary Source History*. Gareth Stevens Publishing, 2005.

Sheehan, Sean. *War in the Pacific (Documenting the War)*. Rosen Central, 2008.

Stolley, Richard B. *LIFE: World War II: History's Greatest Conflict in Pictures*. Bulfinch, 2005.

Ward, Geoffrey C., and Ken Burns. *The War: An Intimate History, 1941–1945*. Knopf, 2007.

Williams, Barbara. *World War II: Pacific*. Lerner Publications, 2004.

Websites

www.worldwar-2.net
A complete World War II timeline, detailing events day by day.

www.secondworldwar.co.uk
A general World War II resource, including important dates, casualty figures, high commands, and trivia.

www.ibiblio.org/pha
A collection of primary World War II source materials.

www.grolier.com/wwii/ wwii_mainpage.html
The story of the war, biographies and articles, photographs, and films.

www.war-experience.org
The Second World War Experience Center.

Index